Bygone Oban

Bernard Byrom

Another mid-nineteenth century view showing the Oban Hotel, which dates from 1790, among the buildings above the outline of the North Pier. Further to the right, along the shore road there was the Steam Packet & Coach Office, the Albert Hotel, George Hotel, William Cumstie & Sons' wine and spirit merchants and the Caledonian Hotel.

OBAN for Ever

SPRING — SUMMER — AUTUMN — WINTER

© Bernard Byrom, 2018
First published in the United Kingdom, 2018,
by Stenlake Publishing Ltd.
www.stenlake.co.uk
ISBN 978-1-84033-807-2

The publishers regret that they cannot supply
copies of any pictures featured in this book.

Printed by
Blissetts, Roslin Road, Acton, W3 8DH

Further Reading

The following were the principal books and websites used by author during his research. None of the books are available from Stenlake Publishing; please contact your local bookshop, reference library or search for them on the internet.

Charles Hunter, *Oban Past and Present*, 1993
Christopher J. Uncles, *Oban and the Land of Lorn*, 2001
Alexander Smith, *A Summer in Skye*, 1865
Baedeker's Great Britain, 1890
National Gazetteer of Great Britain and Ireland, 1863
Sydney Morning Herald
oldglasgowpubs.co.uk
findmypast.co.uk
scotlandsplaces.gov.uk

Acknowledgements

The author would like to thank Mr Peter Smith of Oban War & Peace Museum for his assistance during the research of this book.

Introduction

In 1863 the *National Gazetteer of Great Britain and Ireland* described Oban in these words: 'It is a small town of about 2,000 inhabitants, but promises to be a place of considerable trade as a mart for the western Highlands and the middle district of the Western Isles. The streets are regular, but the houses in general small. The only public buildings are the Custom House and Post Office but there are two convenient piers. The port is chiefly frequented by fishing boats and coastal vessels (the latter importing coal, and exporting grain and whisky) and by several steamers in the summer conveying tourists from this place to Staffa, Iona and the Caledonian Canal. There is a church, Free and United Presbyterian churches, Independent and Episcopalian chapels.'

By this time Oban had already been well established as a tourist transit stop for more than forty years. A new road from Connell had been opened in 1832 and there was a daily coach connection to Inveraray. Ships had been sailing from Glasgow via the Crinan Canal and onwards to Fort William and to Inverness via the Caledonian Canal since the 1820s and from around that time the Highlands had become a romantic destination for those attracted by the area's history and natural beauty. Sir Walter Scott visited the town in 1814, followed by the composer Felix Mendelssohn who visited the Hebrides in 1829, the artist Joseph Mallord William Turner in 1830 and the poet William Wordsworth in 1833. Their works inspired thousands of people to follow in their footsteps and many new hotels were built in Oban to accommodate them. But these travellers never actually *holidayed* in Oban. The situation was explained succinctly by Alexander Smith in his book *A Summer in Skye* which was published in 1865, when he stated that the two requirements of every visitor to Oban were a bed for the night and the time of the steamer. He went on to write: 'From the pier the bell of the departing steamer urges passengers to make haste … people seldom stay there above a night. The tourist no more thinks of spending a week in Oban than he thinks of spending a week in a railway station.' How things have changed today!

The principal hotels built to accommodate the Victorian tourists began with the Caledonian in 1830, followed by the King's Arms in 1855 (rebuilt in 1888), the Great Western in 1862, the Station in 1881 (enlarged in 1886), the Alexandra in 1871, the Grand in 1876 and the Royal in 1895. There were also several temperance hotels in the town. By 1890 the two most luxurious and expensive hotels were the Great Western and the Alexandra, both of which charged 5/6d for accommodation, 3/- for breakfast and 5/- for dinner.

The first proper pier – the South Pier – was constructed in 1814 by the Duke of Argyll to handle the increasing number of boats laden with tourists who wished to experience for themselves the romance of the Highlands and the Inner Hebridean islands of Mull, Staffa and Iona. But this pier proved inadequate for the volume of traffic and by 1846 the North Pier had been constructed by dint of sinking the hulls of derelict ships. Until the 1960s (and after it had been properly reconstructed), it was the primary landing pier for most vessels sailing into and out of Oban and it is still used today.

The railway arrived in 1880 and built its own pier on land reclaimed from the sea. At first it was used primarily by fishing vessels because the goods sidings were alongside, but from the 1960s MacBrayne ferries began using it because of the sheer volume of traffic in the harbour. In 2000 the pier was extended and a substantial new terminal building with a linkspan was constructed to handle what were now CalMac (Caledonian MacBrayne) ferries. Then, in 2006, a second linkspan was constructed so that two ferries could berth and load simultaneously. A linkspan is a device that enables road vehicles to drive from a pier directly into the car deck of a ferry and similarly disembark at their destination.

The arrival of the railway, followed by touring coach parties in the twentieth century and then private cars from the 1950s, enabled many more tourists from southern parts to come to the town and many of these were happy to stay for a week or longer, using their hotel as a base for touring the area. Visitors from abroad now make up a significant part of the summer tourism scene and today's visitors can feel just as inspired as the Victorians when they enjoy watching a beautiful sunset over the isle of Kerrera with the hills of Mull in the background.

A street-level view looking up at the tower that was built by John Stuart McCaig at his own expense. He was a wealthy merchant banker and leading citizen of the town and his philanthropic aim was to give work to local stonemasons who were unemployed during the winter months. In 1875 he purchased Battery Hill above the town, so-called because it had formerly held the guns of the Argyllshire Artillery Volunteers. Constructed of granite from the Bonawe quarries, the tower's walls are over two feet thick and its circumference is about 210 yards. It has an entry arch with two windows above it; in the lower tier there are 44 windows whilst in the top there are 50. Work began in 1896 and McCaig intended not only to add a further storey but to surmount it with statues of himself, his father, mother, brothers and sisters. His will stipulated that these were to cost not less that £1,000 each, would be modelled in either bronze or stone and their likenesses were to be taken from photographs of his family; moreover, the work was to be carried out by young Scottish artists and sculptors. However, after McCaig died in 1902 his sister successfully challenged his will and the tower, which was reputed to have cost him around £5,000 (over £400,000 in today's money), was left in its present unfinished state. For many years its interior was a wilderness but in the twenty-first century gardens have been laid out and the views from the tower over the town and across the bay are unsurpassed.

ARGYLE SQUARE, OBAN

Argyll Square is nowadays a large and very busy road junction in the centre of Oban. The Royal Hotel was built in 1895 and replaced the earlier hotel of the same name that had stood on the opposite side of the square. This earlier hotel had previously been named the New Inn and must have been a good hotel because it was where the Duchess of Orleans and her entourage took seventeen rooms when she visited in 1851, accompanying the ex-queen of France. The hotel was promptly renamed the Royal Hotel and lasted until 1888 when it was demolished. The monument standing in the middle of the square in the form of a mercat-cross-cum-drinking-fountain was erected in 1904 in memory of Dr Robert McKelvie, who endowed an isolation hospital for infectious diseases which was opened in 1896. The white-painted shops on Combie Street are just beyond the square where Aird's Crescent and Stevenson Street join from the left and Lochside Street from the right. This picture shows the square in 1926; since then, the tall five-storey building on the right of the picture has been demolished and replaced by a modern one of four storeys. Otherwise, apart from the loss of their chimneys, the buildings are virtually unchanged today. The shop next to the five-storey building is Forbes' Glasgow Warehouse which sold carpets and general drapery.

This is a 1930s photograph of Stevenson Street at its junction with Hill Street which enters from the bottom left and a minor road which winds up the hill to the church standing on the higher ground. This is the Free High Church in Rockfield Road which was built by David Cousin in 1846 in a light early-Gothic style to the design of Augustus Welby Pugin who did much to revive Gothic architecture in England. John Ruskin described it as one of the most dignified churches in Scotland. The ruins at the crest of the hill are of the ill-fated Hydropathic. The black hut in the foreground was a weighing station; the free public weighbridge can be seen in the roadway in front of the hut, but both are long gone. The mainly wood-built shops on the right came to a fiery end one night in the mid-1950s when a gas canister exploded in Kate's fish shop and set the whole terrace alight. One of the premises was a paint shop which burned briskly and more gas canisters caught fire in a plumber's store, the resulting explosion throwing two firemen off the roof. The buildings have been rebuilt in stone and are now the premises of Ladbrokes bookmakers. The large ecclesiastical-looking building (though it was never a church) in the middle of the picture is nowadays the premises of Oban Electrical Services Ltd whilst the legal firm of Stevenson Kennedy occupy the upper floor.

The coming of the railway to Oban in 1880 resulted in a large increase in tourism to the area and the following year a group of mainly Glasgow shareholders formed the Oban Hills Hydropathic & Sanatorium Company. Hydropathy was a method of treating diseases using pure water both internally and externally; the method was very popular for several decades during the nineteenth century and hydropathic establishments sprang up all over the country. In Oban a site was acquired high above the town and grandiose plans were drawn up for a building in the Scots Baronial style that would have 137 bedrooms, a conservatory, concert hall and sea water baths. Externally there would be stables, workshops, a golf course and a funicular railway to transport guests and their luggage to and from the town, station and steamer pier. An initial estimated cost of £75,000 (£6.4 million in today's money) was deemed too expensive and it was revised downwards to an impossibly low £32,000 (£2.72 million). The contract was given to the firm of Robert McAlpine & Company who assigned 300 workmen to the project. Work progressed rapidly and the building had risen three storeys to roof height with the roof timbers in place when the money ran out towards the end of the following year, 1882. The shareholders were either unable or unwilling to invest more capital and work ceased that winter. It was never resumed and the building, despite being almost structurally complete, was abandoned. Over the years its stonework was pillaged to build the villas that sprang up in the neighbourhood and its ruins became ever more reduced in size and gaunt in appearance. For many years they were visible from the town (see the preceding picture) but are nowadays invisible behind the trees that have grown up on the hillside.

An Edwardian vista of Queen's Park Place, seen from the railway station forecourt with the Station Hotel in the foreground and a small range of little shops attached, headed by R. Drummond's silversmiths and lapidaries. Drummond's is nowadays the Iona jewellery shop and the end building is the West Coast Motors' shop for booking tours around the area and to the isles. From behind the hotel George Street runs into the distance past a range of hotels including the King's Arms, Bay View Temperance and Caledonian hotels. The tall chimney is at the Oban Distillery in Stafford Street and the round tower peeping above the rooftops on the left of the picture belongs to the large house in Dalriach Road named Greystones which is now a boutique bed and breakfast establishment.

Destruction Of Queen's Hotel Oban. Oct 24th 1924

The Queen's Hotel, built in 1891, occupied a site on the corner of George Street and Stevenson Street on the other side of the Railway Hotel. Early on the morning of 24 October 1924 a railway clerk on his way to work discovered it to be on fire and, having raised the alarm at the hotel, he alerted the Police Station in Albany Street. Around the same time the commander of a naval survey ship standing off Oban Bay also noticed that the hotel was on fire and he landed blue-jackets to assist in rescue work and attracted others to help by means of firing rocket signals. The hotel was busy at the time and most of the guests, who were asleep when the fire began, were rescued before the staircase collapsed but four women servants were cut off on the top floor, 40 feet up, which the longest available ladder failed to reach. A blue-jacket mounted the top rung of the ladder and jumped upwards onto the balcony, then he lowered the four women individually by means of a rope. Finally, he attached the rope to the building and climbed down it to safety. The hotel was gutted by the fire but the building itself was subsequently rebuilt.

In 1928 the Royal Bank of Scotland relocated into these newly-rebuilt premises of the former Queen's Hotel on George Street. Later still they relocated again, this time a little further along the street into the premises of the National Commercial Bank of Scotland after the two banks merged in 1969. Ground floor shops in this 1930s picture include Rankin's Gift House and a chemist, while next along are the Palace Hotel, King's Arms Hotel and the Caledonian Hotel. The darker domed building of Chalmers Highland Tweed House is visible on the far side of Argyll Street.

Four immaculate carriages and their drivers await business outside the King's Arms Hotel in the late afternoon of a lovely summer's day. Nowadays the structure has lost its impressive tower. The building on the right of the picture was the premises of the National Commercial Bank of Scotland (previously the National Bank of Scotland) and is now occupied by their eventual successor, the Royal Bank of Scotland. No fewer than five temperance hotels are visible on the other side of the hotel and there were others not in the picture; not one such establishment survives in Oban today. The two nearest temperance hotels on the far side of Argyll Street were later replaced by Argyll Mansions.

Another Edwardian view looking along George Street northwards from Queen's Park Place. The two smaller buildings between the Caledonian Hotel and the King's Arms Hotel are McNeill's Railway Temperance Hotel and the Bay View Temperance Hotel. Both have shops on the ground floor, as have the buildings across the road on the North Pier. There is yet another temperance hotel on the corner next to the Commercial Hotel. These buildings are nowadays professional offices. The rooftop sign saying 'Marine' is advertising the presence of the Marine Hotel which is out of sight on the Corran Esplanade beyond the North Pier.

Carnival Day At Oban.

Carnival day at Oban sometime around 1930 with the cavalcade passing along George Street past Argyll Mansions and the Caledonian Hotel. The leading vehicle is a 1920s 'Bullnose' Morris with a Glasgow registration plate, carrying the inscription on its windscreen: 'The Maharajah of Outdore, and Miss Mancy Niller' (sic). The two shops of James Hutton and G.A. Macleod are currently the premises of Boots Pharmacy and New Look women's fashions.

An Edwardian view of George Street at its crossroads with Stafford Street. The Imperial Hotel is now the Cuan Mor restaurant and bar whilst Kerchar's Family Grocer's shop next door with Livingston's Temperance Hotel above it is now the Mountain Warehouse. Next to that is the George Hotel followed by the imposing sandstone building named Argyll Mansions and then Argyll Street itself. The George is now divided between the Whisky Shop and the Nationwide Building Society whilst the ground floor of Argyll Mansions now houses W.H. Smith and Chalmers Highland Tweed House. The facades of both the Temperance Hotel and the George Hotel are unrecognisable today but the biggest loss from the picture is the Caledonian Hotel on the other side of Argyll Street: it has been replaced by a two-storey building housing the Edinburgh Woollen Mill and the Oban Bay Fish Bar with the Skipinnish Ceilidh Night Club above them on the first floor. In its time the Caledonian was one of the best hotels in the town and when the ex-queen of France visited Oban in 1851 the hotel placed 27 rooms at her disposal. Beyond the Caledonian are two small shops with McNeill's Railway Temperance Hotel and the Bay View Temperance Hotel above them, then comes the King's Arms Hotel which is nowadays the King's Arms Holiday Apartments with a branch of Superdrug on the ground floor.

14

This is a similar view to the previous picture but taken from ground level. Sadly, the ornate cast iron public drinking fountain in the foreground has been replaced by a concrete traffic island to facilitate traffic negotiating the town centre's one-way system.

27. Oban From The Harbour

This photograph dates from 1922. The Oban Distillery was built in 1794 by the entrepreneurial brothers Hugh and John Stevenson and is nowadays best known for its limited range of premium single malt whiskies. It's tall chimney, for many years a landmark in the town, has since been shortened. The large building on the corner of George Street and Stafford Street, once a branch of the City of Glasgow Bank, bears the name of New Apothecary's Hall on its wall and was occupied by Robertson the chemist. It is now a Specsavers' shop. The Craig-Ard Hotel on the hillside has been the Craigard Self-Catering Apartments since April 2015.

The Congregational church in Tweedale Street was built in 1880 on the site of an older church but the congregation was founded as far back as 1805. At that time, the fellowship became known as the 'Oban Independent Church' and it met with great opposition from the established church, local landowners and some local inhabitants. Preaching was done from a rock on the shore and the members of the congregation were sometimes chased and pelted with stones by members of the Established Church. The architect for this building was Alexander Shairp and it is modelled on an Alexander 'Greek' Thomson design. It is built of yellow sandstone with zinc windows which is quite unusual for this area. This has caused problems because the stone is very porous and the zinc and lead are too soft. By 2004 the building needed major refurbishment inside and out and the congregation embarked upon a restoration project. Two years later the church was fully restored, the vestry renovated and the undercroft redesigned. The turned stone balusters and forestairs to the entrance door were repaired and the roof was re-slated and insulated. In addition, three cast iron and twelve badly decayed zinc windows were restored. Apart from the removal of the railings the building looks exactly the same today as in the picture. The building on the right used to be the church hall and is now shared between local branches of the Sea Cadets and the Air Training Corps.

This picture shows the late-Gothic style St John's Episcopal Church as originally built in 1864 with the addition of a south nave in 1882. The building was aligned east-west with its east gable facing onto what is now George Street and owed its existence to the generosity of two local lairds, McDougall of Dunollie and Campbell of Dunstaffnage, who paid for the building plot.

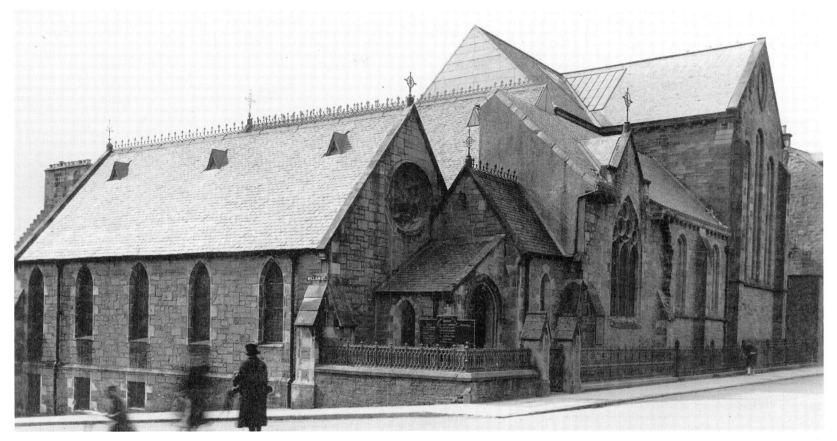

Bishop Chinnery-Haldane, who was elected in 1883, had plans drawn up for a much larger St John's church and after his death in 1906 the idea was raised once more as a memorial to him. The Glasgow architect James Chalmers won a competition to design the new church and work began in 1908. However, when money ran out in August 1910 only the sanctuary, chancel, one transept and one bay of the nave had been completed, leaving a considerable part of the intended structure unbuilt. The alignment of the new church was turned through 90 degrees to align north-south and had a floor level 12 feet higher than the older part. In 1920 this enlarged church, now called St John the Divine, became a cathedral and the seat of the Episcopal Bishop of Argyll and The Isles. Although plans have been drawn up from time to time to complete the work on the church structure, it is still largely as it was when work stopped in 1910. Inside the building two large riveted steel buttresses and other steelwork have been inserted into the roof to ensure the stability of what was actually built, and the faces of the disciples painted on the reredos above the high altar are the faces of members of the 1910 congregation. This picture shows the enlarged church, seen from the same angle in George Street as in the previous picture.

This building at the northern end of George Street at its junction with Nursery Lane began life on a smaller scale during the First World War as the West Highland Sailors' and Soldiers' Rest. One of its customers was a Royal Navy seaman with a great interest in photography; his name was Henry Morton Scrivens and he thought it would make an ideal studio for his work. After his discharge from the navy at the end of the war he purchased the building and named it the 'Maison de Photographie'. With the return of tourists his business flourished but he also did an immense amount of freelance photography, especially for the Oban Times, and also produced postcards of local places. He extended the building to its size in the picture and in its heyday the business employed a staff of fourteen. When he retired in 1958 and his business ceased trading, his large stock of negatives were stored at the *Oban Times'* premises but when the *Times* subsequently moved to more modern premises most of his photographic plates were unfortunately damaged or destroyed. His premises are still recognisable, albeit in a somewhat altered form, and are currently the Taj Mahal Restaurant and takeaway.

In 1843 the Established (Presbyterian) Church in Scotland was riven by a dispute over patronage that resulted in dissidents creating a Free Church of Scotland. Very soon this Free Church itself became riven by theological disputes amongst its own members and itself fragmented, resulting in even more variants and churches, all calling themselves the Free Church. In Oban matters were further complicated because services were conducted in Gaelic whereas English visitors wished to hear them conducted in English, resulting in them building their own church in Argyll Square on the corner of Albany Street. In 1900 a number of these splinter groups joined together and then amalgamated with the mainstream Free Church to form the United Free Church of Scotland. When this in turn united with the established Church of Scotland in 1929 Oban found itself with no fewer than four churches of the same denomination, each with its own congregation. Inevitably there had to be rationalisation and there is nowadays only one active Church of Scotland church in Oban. The United Free church in this 1908 picture is one such casualty; it was built in 1867–68 at the top end of George Street to a design by John McKillop and claimed the distinction of having Benjamin Disraeli as a worshipper during his visit to Oban in 1872. It stands at the junction of Dunollie Road and Breadalbane Street and has been a commercial premises since the 1980s. Nowadays it is shorn of its steeple and further disguised by the addition of a sloping extension that runs from the frontage round to the right-hand side. The front of the building is nowadays the premises of Matrix Computers and a backpacker's hostel occupies the rest of the building.

The Marine Hotel, seen here in 1916, was built by Major McCaig at the start of the Corran Esplanade. It is four storeys high plus an attic, built in the Scots Baronial style of sandstone with ashlar dressings and features crow-stepped gables with a pepperpot turret. Opened in 1896 to provide accommodation of the very highest class, it was built, fitted up and furnished without regard to expense and contained every modern convenience. The Drawing Room was furnished in Chippendale mahogany and the Writing Room had cathedral glass windows. Comfortable rooms were also provided on the top floor for the guests' servants who accompanied them. The building on the left was originally Major McCaig's own house.

In 1936 Major McCaig's house was demolished and the Marine Hotel was extended to the left by James Taylor in painted concrete in a contemporary building style. It was connected to the original hotel by bridges at first and fourth floor levels; the dining room was situated on the ground floor to the left of the hotel sign and its entrance was up a curved stair to a terrace with a glass-roofed canopy displaying the hotel's name. Since then the hotel's name has been changed to 'Regent Hotel' and the building has been further heightened by the addition of two more storeys including a mansard roof. Nowadays the main entrance to the hotel is up the curved stair. Both the round canopy over the ground-level entrance and the 'drum' gate piers with the globe lamps have been removed and the 'Marine Hotel' sign has been replaced by 'Regent Hotel'.

ESPLANADE LOOKING EAST, OBAN

An interesting view looking back along the Corran esplanade. The hoardings attached to the railings outside the Esplanade Boarding House (no relation to the Esplanade Hotel nearer to the town centre) are displaying advertisements for the rival routes to Scotland offered by the Midland Railway (via the Settle and Carlisle line and offering express trains with breakfast, dining and sleeping cars) and the east coast route via York, Berwick and Edinburgh operated by the Great Northern, North Eastern and North British Railway companies. On the left the Highland Railway is advertising its hotels at Inverness, Dornoch and Kyle of Lochalsh and other advertisements and posters abound. The Esplanade Boarding House is now the West Bay Holiday Apartments. Beyond the Great Western Hotel is the Park Hotel and then the unsightly end of St John's Cathedral after its west window had been sealed following the church's rebuilding in 1910. Beyond it is a former bank with the date of 1871 inscribed in stone on its gable; it is now the Coasters pub.

These two pictures show two stages in the enlargement of the Park Hotel on the south side of the Great Western Hotel. Whatever may be said about the architecture of the new extension it did at least hide the unsightly end of St John's Cathedral in the previous picture! Note that the smaller building on the left now displays an 'Esplanade Hotel' sign whereas on the previous picture it bears the 'Park Hotel' sign.

In due course the Esplanade Hotel was modernised, enlarged and given a new façade but was destroyed by fire on 24 March 1973. The alarm was raised when a sailor on his yacht in Oban Bay saw a glow in the first-floor reception area of the hotel at about 3.15 a.m. He sent one of his crew ashore to raise the alarm and also sounded his foghorn. The *Daily Record* reported that 'The tragedy began around 4 a.m. when what was suspected to be a 'dropped light' was discarded and the building caught fire. Within minutes the blaze spread through the five-storey building – which had recently been refurbished – and many guests were trapped in their rooms. Some clung to window ledges. A ladder that hadn't been used for seventeen years snapped and two firemen were catapulted onto an outhouse roof. The owner, Ian Nicholson, said he had been advised to carry out extensive modifications but had postponed them because of the cost. Ten middle-aged and elderly people died, all from a coach party from England'. The building on the left of the picture is still there and forms part of the Great Western Hotel but the Esplanade Hotel itself and the adjoining Park Hotel have been demolished and replaced by a large block of modern holiday apartments named Esplanade Court.

ESPLANADE HOTEL OBAN.

The Great Western Hotel was built in 1862 to the designs of Charles Wilson of Glasgow and has been cited as the finest example of surviving Victorian hotel architecture in the town. In 1882 a grand dining room to seat 200 people was added to the rear of the hotel and in 1884 it became the first hotel in Oban to have electric lighting installed. It was built to be a luxury hotel and was the place to stay and be seen during the annual Argyllshire Gathering. In common with certain other large hotels in the town (the Marine, Park and Esplanade) it was requisitioned by the Royal Air Force during the Second World War and was used as their local headquarters until 1945. It is nowadays known as the Bay Great Western Hotel and is part of the 'Bay' group of hotels owned by Shearing's holiday company.

22611 The Harbour & Railway Station. Oban

A busy scene at Oban Harbour early in the twentieth century with ships moored at the North Pier on the extreme left of the picture, several at various berths at the Railway Pier in the centre and one at the South Pier in the foreground. The long lines of Caledonian Railway carriages in the station and sidings show how busy the railway was during the summer months. The Callander & Oban Railway was authorised in 1865 and construction began the following year but shortage of money meant that the line had to be built in stages and it wasn't until 1880 that it eventually reached Oban. A new landing pier was built on reclaimed land and the company also built an elegant passenger station with a glazed covered roof over some of the platforms and a clock tower incorporated into the façade. The railway's arrival was celebrated by a huge banquet held in the station hall on 30 June. Unhappily the station was rebuilt in 1987 and the clock tower and platform roof were swept away, to be replaced with a modern building.

A striking view from Pulpit Hill of the shops and hotels along Oban's waterfront and the villas on the hillside with the legendary cruise ship *King George V* moored at the Railway Pier. In 1925 Turbine Steamers Limited had ordered her from William Denny & Brothers of Dumbarton. A revolutionary design, she was powered by six steam turbines and was licensed to carry 814 passengers. Brought into service in 1926, her regular run was initially from Glasgow's Prince's Pier to Inveraray and back via Dunoon, Rothesay and Tighnabruaich. In 1935 the company was taken over by MacBrayne's who soon put her on the Sacred Isles tour from Oban to Staffa and Iona, with which she was synonymous for the rest of her sailing career. She was withdrawn from this service in 1974 and was sold to Nationwide Transport who left her sitting in a dry dock at Cardiff for six years before selling her to Bass Charrington Ltd. They intended to convert her into a floating restaurant moored at the Thames Embankment in London but she suffered a serious fire on 26 August 1981 while being refurbished and after a further three years her remains were beached opposite Penarth and abandoned to the waves, a sad end for a lovely ship.

The former Piermaster's House in the foreground, now used by the local branch of the RNLI, was built around 1814 and is one of the oldest buildings in Oban. It is located at the end of the South Pier. The hills above the town are crowned by the proud circle of McCaig's Tower on the left and the melancholy remains of the Hydropathic on the right. The tall church spire just to the right of the ship's foremast is that of the former St Columba's Free Church of Scotland at the bottom of Albany Street in Argyll Square. It was built in 1888 partly on the site of the old Royal Hotel at a cost of £3,600 (£330,000 in today's money), accommodated 500 worshipers and was designed in the Gothic style by local architect John Fraser Sim. Its 128 feet high steeple was reduced in size in 1976 and the church closed in 1984 after the congregation merged with St Columba's U.P. Church. The building first became a nightclub and then the local tourist office but is nowadays empty and advertised for sale.

8044 OBAN. AT THE OLD PIER. — JUDGES LTD

Glasgow-registered trawler GW18 is moored at the South Pier adjacent to the former Piermaster's House. She was built in 1907 by Alexander Hall & Sons Limited of Aberdeen for John Stuart Boyle of Glasgow but in 1914 she was requisitioned by the Admiralty and converted to a minesweeper based at Dover for the duration of the First World War. In 1926 she was registered to Aberdeen owners as A.177 and remained based there until 1937 when she was sold for scrap to Metal Industries Limited of Charlestown, Fife.

A collection of fishing boats at the South Pier making ready to go back to sea, judging from the smoke from their funnels. The registration letters on their bows and funnels indicate that they include vessels from Inverness, Banff, Fraserburgh and Peterhead, all on the other side of Scotland.

When the Callander & Oban Railway arrived in Oban in 1880 they built sidings and a landing pier alongside the passenger station. This became known as the Railway Pier and it immediately began to attract the Stornoway fish traffic away from the Highland Railway and their landing ports further north. The catch was principally herring but white fish and lobsters were also landed. The herring were lifted from the ships in wicker baskets, each of which held about 6 stone (84 lbs or 38 kilos) of fish and four baskets made up a 'cran'. This was a unit of measure of landed uncleaned herring and a standard wooden box held an average of 1,200 fish. An army of gutters known as the Herring Lassies followed the shoals of herring around the country from Stornoway in the north to Yarmouth in East Anglia. This is a photograph of herring being landed at the Railway Pier in 1928. Wooden boxes lined with ice were packed with gutted fish at the quayside and overnight express fish trains ran to London and southern markets. Most of the wooden boxes in the picture bear the name of John Burgon; this firm was founded in Eyemouth in 1906 and later became one of the leading European crab processors.

The *Hebrides* was built in 1898 for John MacCallum as a cargo ship with passenger accommodation and offered leisurely cruises around the Western Isles including St Kilda. She was reboilered in 1937, taken over by MacBrayne's in 1948 and survived until 1955 when she was replaced by *Loch Ard*. In her final years she carried cargo and livestock only, on her old route from Glasgow. She was scrapped at Smith & Company, Port Glasgow, and her ship's bell is now on display in the lounge of the present-day Caledonian MacBrayne ferry *Hebrides*.

A Morris Minor car being hoisted aboard *Lochearn* in July 1957 from the pier at Oban en route to Mull. Until the first side-loading ferries with hydraulic lifts were introduced in 1963–64 this was the only way of transporting a vehicle to and from the islands. The car was driven onto a large net, stuffed sacking protectors were attached and then the load was lifted bodily by the ship's derrick and deposited on the ship where it was secured on the open deck. Side-loading ships were superseded in turn from the 1970s by the modern 'Roll-On-Roll-Off' (RO-RO) ferries which can be loaded via a linkspan through either the bow or the stern and the vehicle driven straight off over a corresponding linkspan at the other end. The popular Oban–Craignure (Mull) service is nowadays usually operated by *Isle of Mull* which was launched in 1987 and has space for 80 cars.

With the North Pier and Columba Hotel as a backdrop the Morris Minor has been secured on deck. *Lochearn* was built in 1930 and replaced *Lochinvar* as the MacBrayne mail steamer serving Barra and South Uist until 1955 when she was replaced in turn by *Claymore*. She then became the Sound of Mull mail steamer between Oban, Salen, Lochaline, Craignure and Tobermory until 1964, after which she was sold to Greek owners and was converted at Pireaus into a private motor yacht named *Naias*. It is believed that she was broken up in January 1975.

This picture shows a helicopter on the landing pad at the Northern Lighthouse Board's depot on Gallenach Road in 1974. The Board is responsible for marine navigation aids around the coastal areas of the British Isles and was formed by an Act of Parliament in 1786 for the initial purpose of building four Scottish lighthouses. These were at Kinnaird Head, North Ronaldsay, Scalpay and Mull of Kintyre and all had been completed by October 1789. Many other lighthouses followed, the majority of them built by the famous Stevenson family of lighthouse builders, and several were in extremely challenging locations such as those at the Bell Rock, Skerryvore and Muckle Flugga. Technical operations are nowadays carried out at this base in Oban where there are maintenance workshops and facilities for the construction of buoys and beacons, and its vessels are also based here. The helicopter is needed to transfer personnel to and from remote sites around the coast of Scotland and the Isle of Man for lighthouse maintenance. The large building on the Corran Esplanade is St Columba's Roman Catholic Cathedral which is built of granite and was designed by Sir Giles Gilbert Scott who was also architect of the huge Anglican cathedral at Liverpool. Their original church had been built in 1886 from sections of corrugated iron but had been beautifully furnished. Work on its replacement started in 1932 but was interrupted by the Second World War; however, work was resumed after the war and the cathedral was opened in 1959. The largely fifteenth century ruins of Dunollie Castle can be seen on the extreme left of the picture.

This large rock on the shoreline at the south end of Dungallan Park in Gallenach Road is known locally as the Brandy Stone and probably fell from the cliffs above at some time in the distant past. Its name is supposed to derive from the time in the eighteenth century when the locals smuggled brandy rather than pay the exorbitant excise duty on it. This is a very sheltered part of the bay and the area around the rock was a good place to land and hide the contraband liquor.

Monzievard Boarding House, Oban.

This house is situated on Gallanach Road at its junction with Glenmore Road and near the Brandy Stone. It is now a private house but is instantly recognisable as the former Monzievaird Boarding House.

Oban.

Burrows Ship-Yard On Fire, Feb 9th 1921.

The engineering and shipbuilding yard of Messrs Burrows and Company at Gallanach, south of Oban, was built around the turn of the twentieth century. During the First World War it was under government control and a considerable amount of work was carried out on drifters and trawlers on naval service. Around 2 a.m. on the morning of 9 February 1921 the yard was discovered to be on fire and several motor boats that had been laid up in the launch store for the winter were destroyed. Local people were able to prevent the fire from spreading to a neighbouring cottage and an adjoining portable shed.

A glass-making factory was opened in 1970 in the Lochavuillin area of Oban to produce paperweights and other glass products. These photographs of the workshop and an employee working colour strips into glass blobs both date from 1971.

Far right: Another photograph from 1971, of the showroom tables at the glassworks factory. Under its later ownership by Caithness Glass, a retail shop was opened in 1992 on the Oban waterfront development on the Railway Pier but the factory at Lochavuillin was closed in 1995. Caithness Glass sold their business in 2002 to Royal Worcester and Spode who closed the Oban retail shop in 2004 when Caithness Glass went into receivership. Currently Caithness Glass is owned by Dartington Crystal and since 2007 it has had a small glassmaking operation at the visitor centre in Crieff.

In 1903 the Duke of Argyll opened the new road to Ganavan which extended the northern part of the promenade known as The Plateau at the far end of Dunollie Esplanade. Ganavan Sands is a beautiful stretch of sands in Ganavan Bay, about 2 miles north of Oban town centre, overlooking the Sound of Kerrera with views across the Lynn of Lorne to Lismore and the mountains of Mull. Brightly-coloured wooden beach chalets and bathers' windbreaks adorn the bathing beach in this photograph.

New Pavilion, Ganavan Sands, Oban. H.M.S.

A wooden tea room originally stood here but was destroyed by fire. It was replaced by this stylish new pavilion on the south side of the sands in the 1930s but this was demolished in 2007 to make way for a development of luxury homes. Now there is only a little kiosk selling drinks and snacks in summer.

A. 5988.

CAMPING GROUND, GANAVAN SANDS, OBAN.

A bird's eye view of Ganavan Sands camping ground in the 1930s. By the 1960s the facilities included a shop, café, children's playground, pitch and putt course and a large caravan and camping site. Now all of this has gone since 2007 when the car park was enlarged into a large pay-and-display facility and the area of the caravan and camping site, together with the site of the 'new' pavilion in the picture, have been covered by houses. Camper vans have replaced the tents.

Ganavan Sands, Oban.

A 1930s photograph of the children's playground at the north end of Ganavan Sands. During the Second World War Sunderland flying boats were maintained and took off from here.

Every year on the fourth Thursday in August Oban hosts the Highland Games, one of the largest in Scotland. These were first proposed in 1871 with a view to holding 'an Annual Gathering of the Gentry of the County of Argyll for social purposes, the Gathering to be called The Argyllshire Gathering, and to be held at such time and place as may hereafter be determined'. The games were held under the presidency of the Duke of Argyll (they still are) and the first ball was held the following year in a hall in Breadalbane Street, a great social event in the town ever since. Dress instructions for men specify Highland Evening Dress, Mess Dress, Hunt Coat or White Tie whilst ladies must wear full length ball gowns. Competitions at the games include throwing the hammer, putting the shot and tossing the caber, as well as traditional athletics. The games' piping competition is also held elsewhere in the town over two days.

Oban Games.   Tossing The Caber.

Tossing the caber is one of the more spectacular 'heavy' events at any Highland Games. A full-sized caber is a tapered pole that is typically 19 feet 6 inches long although its length may vary between 17 feet and 22 feet. The competitor holds the narrower end in their cupped hands and supports the caber against their shoulder as they run forward, then come to a sudden stop as they throw the caber with all their strength and momentum. Their objective is to throw it in such a way that it turns end over end and lands pointing away from them, ideally in the '12 o'clock' position which gains the highest marks.

On a quieter note the staff of Chalmers Highland Tweed Warehouse are enjoying a day out at the Oban tennis courts in 1930. Mr Chalmers is sitting in the centre and the Display Manager, John D.P. Sinclair (with dark hair) is standing on the right in the back row.

Kerrera Ferry, Oban

The island of Kerrera is situated to the west of Oban Bay and shelters it from the westerly winds and gales. Its current population is about 35 persons but in the early 1800s it was around 200. This ferry crossing is situated at Gallenach, about 2 miles south of Oban, and today its modern concrete slipway allows a ferryboat operated by Kerrera Ferries Limited to operate a half-hourly service across the short distance to the island throughout much of the day. The boat only holds twelve passengers per trip but the timetable says that it will return to collect any passengers above this number who had to be left behind. Another delightful note on the timetable states that 'If your journey is time critical for any reason (i.e. bus or train connections) please inform the skipper your journey is urgent'. Not the kind of obliging notice you see on the timetables of larger ferry operators!